Dedication

*To My Heavenly Devin Lee…*
*For all of your love,*
*your courage, and your understanding*
*while we were growing up together.*

by Ronnie Sellers

illustrated by Peggy Jo Ackley

Designer Carlo DeLucia

CAEDMON  New York

*Library of Congress Cataloging in Publication Data*
Sellers, Ronnie, 1948–
If Christmas were a poem.
Summary: Reflects a child's thoughts as she imagines Christmas
as a poem, a song, a time for thanks, and other things.
  [1. Christmas—Fiction]    I. Ackley, Peggy Jo, ill.
II. Title.
PZ7.S456994If    1983    [E]    83-7525

ISBN 0-89845-057-8 Library
      0-89845-164-7
Published by Caedmon, New York
Printed in the U.S.A.    First Edition

10  9  8  7  6  5  4  3  2  1

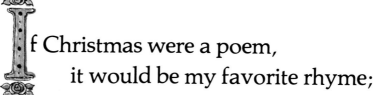

If Christmas were a poem,
      it would be my favorite rhyme;

If Christmas were a song to sing,
I'd sing it all the time;

If Christmas were a painting,
it would be the best to see;

If Christmas were a dancer,

I would have it dance with me.

If Christmas were the season to be merry
     and be bright,
I think I'd take a trip to town and do just
     that one night;
I'd wish a "Merry Christmas!" to each smiling
     face I'd meet,
And it would be such fun to feel the magic
     in the streets!

If Christmas were a small green tree,
I'd cover it with lights,
And decorate its every branch,
until it looked just right;

And then I'd gather all my friends
and serve them tarts and tea,
And tell them all how very much
their friendship means to me.

If Christmas were for giving gifts
  to loved ones close to you,
I'd make a gift for every one
  (there would be quite a few);

On Christmas eve I'd wrap them up and
  place them 'neath the tree—
And try to keep from peeking
  at the gifts left there for me!

If Christmas were a stocking,
 mine would be too large to wear;

If Christmas were a time for thanks,
I'd say a little prayer;

If Santa Claus came sliding down
  *my* chimney Christmas eve,

He'd find so many cookies
  he might never want to leave!

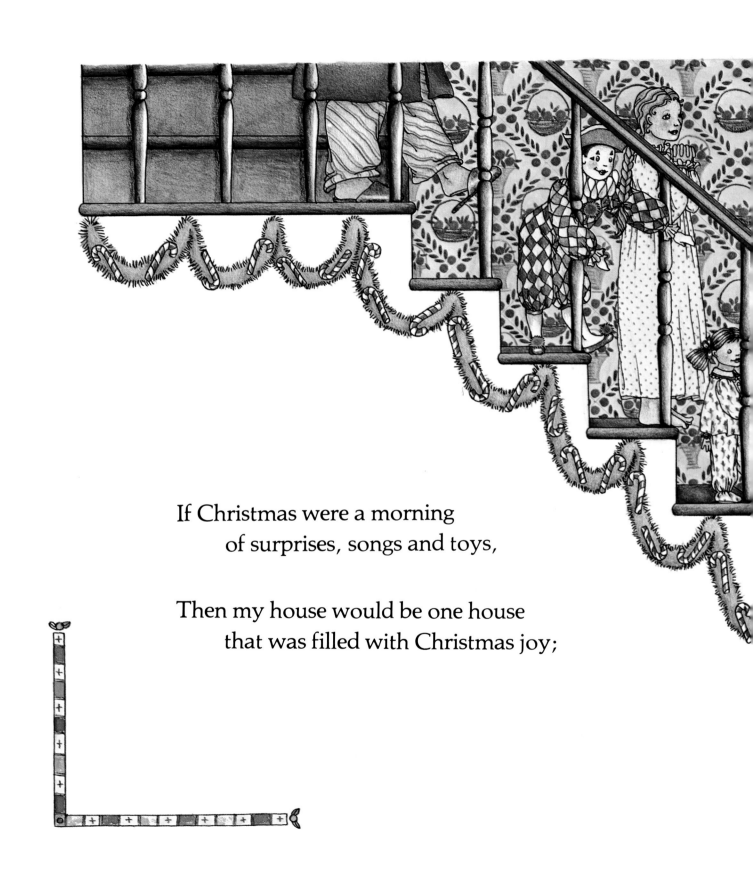

If Christmas were a morning
    of surprises, songs and toys,

Then my house would be one house
    that was filled with Christmas joy;

If Christmas were a day that marked
a very good man's birth,

I'd stop awhile and think of how
He hoped for peace on earth.

If Christmas were a dinner,
	it would be the one I'd make;

If Christmas were a pastry,
    I'd be awfully plump from cake!

If Christmas were a puppy,
    I would hold that puppy tight;

If Christmas were a star,
  I'd wish upon it every night.

But Christmas isn't just a poem
    or just a melody,

It isn't just a dancer or a puppy
    or a tree;

It's more than just a brilliant star,
    or cakes with extra spice—

It's every special thing at once,
    and that's why it's so nice!